Jack & Emma's
- *adoptee* -
Journey

Written by
Pam Kroskie

Illustrated by
Ashleigh McGill

Written by Pam Kroskie
Illustrated by Ashleigh McGill
Designed by Jeremy Gotwals

Copyright © 2014 Pam Kroskie

No part of this book may be copied or reproduced by any means without the written permission of the author.

For more information about the author visit:
www.JackAndEmmasJourney.com

Published Co-Operatively by Holon Publishing, a Publishing Company, Creative Agency, and artistic community dedicated to the holistic connection between authors, artists, businesess and non-profits.
www.Holonpublishing.com

Printed in the United States of America.

ISBN: 978-0-9915282-0-2

To Leslie Ann -
The special little girl who is my light and soul.

When Jack and Emma get bigger,
they will know their story...

Jack looked in the mirror
and wondered who he looks like.

Adoptees have thoughts and fantasies about their biological families. They wonder if they have siblings, and whether they share a **resemblance**. This is your child searching for their **connection** and **identity**.

Sometimes at school,
Emma gets nervous and worried that
her parents won't be there to pick her up.

Jack thinks about his adoption story, and asks his parents to tell him his story.

The adoptee wants to know as much as you can tell them. It is their **"birth" story** and it helps them form a picture in their mind with the details you can tell them. **It is a comfort to know as much as possible. Every detail helps them for a picture in their mind.**

Some days after school...

... Jack likes to sit down and draw pictures of what he thinks his biological family might look like.

Also, what his house and other surroundings might have been like.

This is a great exercise for the adoptee. Allow your child to sit down and express their thoughts and feelings through drawing.

Jack has a birthday coming up. He feels confused, and wonders if his biological family is thinking of him on his birthday.

This can be a day of loss and anxiety. Some children may withdraw and daydream, while others may be angry and actually sabotage the day.

Some adoptees have attachment needs.
Being away from their mom or dad makes them uneasy and creates a strong need to be in their home - safe, sound, and protected. This is a common reaction. Having openness and honesty, as well as allowing them to discuss their feelings, is important for the child to be able to cope with these emotions.

Emma has gone to stay all night at Grandma's house. She wants to go home, to be close to her mom, because bed time can be scary.

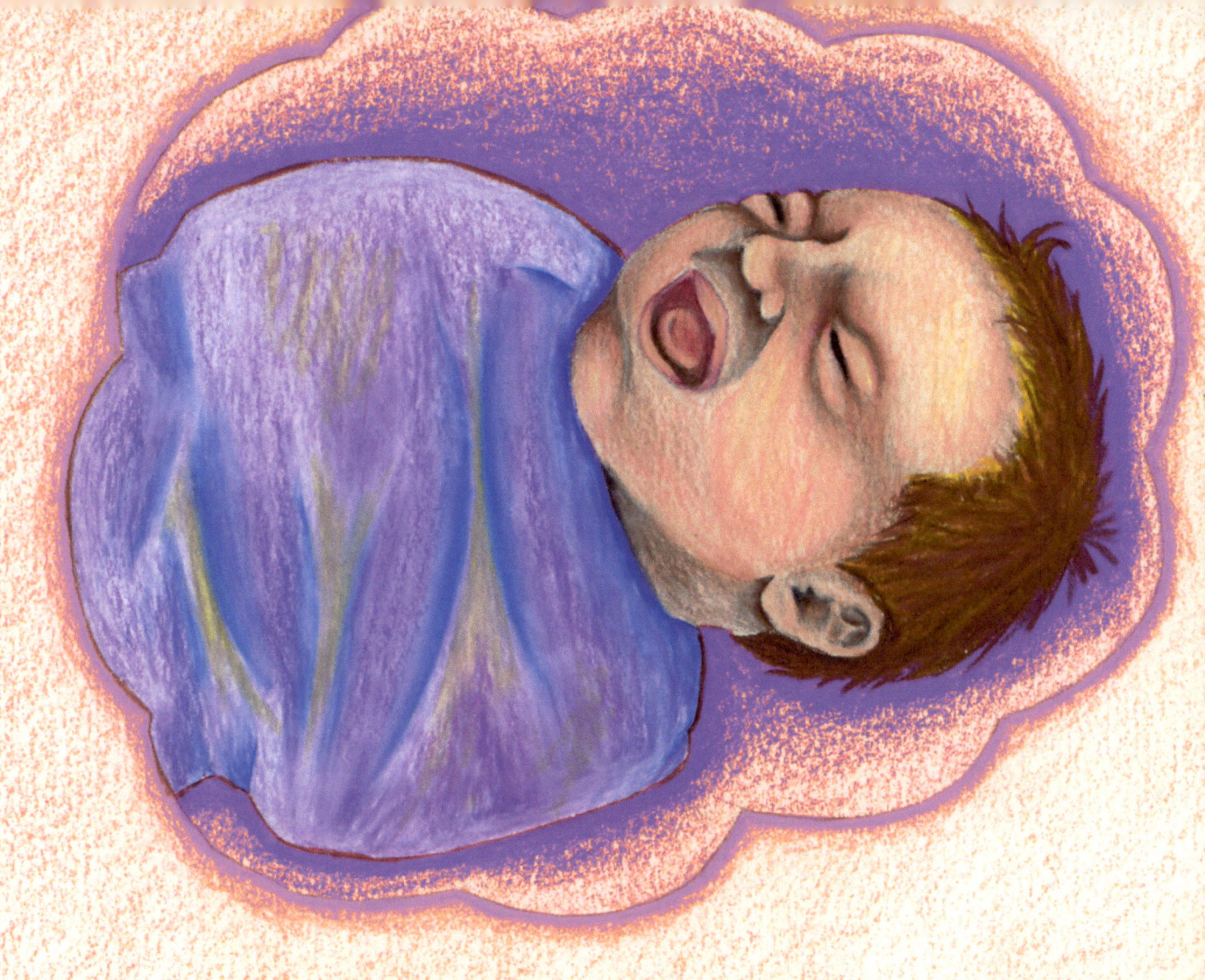

> This is an opportunity to help guide your child through these emotions. Allow your child to express their thoughts and feelings, and follow with positive reinforcement.

There are days that Emma feels overwhelmed, lonely, and not sure how to tell her mom and dad these feelings.

Adopted children will take the lead from their parents on how much, or how little, they talk about being adopted. It is complex, but if you can keep an open dialogue, it will help them express their emotions.

Today, Jack and Emma have been able to talk about their feelings and what it feels like to be adopted. There are all kinds of ways you can express how you feel.
You are an amazing person and just know that each day you have a chance to share your story with people!

Jack and Emma will one day know their story. One day, they will write it."

About the Author

Pam Kroskie is an adoptee who is reunited with her mother and two sisters. Pam was fortunate to have had 22 years with her mother before she passed away from breast cancer. She continues to have a relationship with her amazing sisters and niece and nephews. Pam has three grown sons, Ryan, Seth and Luke who are her pride and joy.

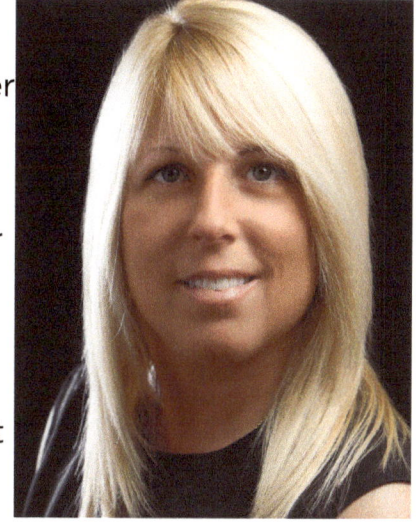

Pam is currently President of the American Adoption Congress, a non-profit that educates and advocates on behalf of all members. There are many positions within the AAC she is also involved with she is the Mid-West Regional Director and the Indiana State Representative. She also hosts a radio show on Blog Talk Radio-called AAC Adoption News and Views.

Pam also received a Congressional Angel in Adoption Award by Congressman Todd Young in 2012. She has also written articles for Adoption Today Magazine.

Pam is also President of her own grassroots organization called H.E.A.R. Hoosiers for Equal Access to Records.

www.ingramcontent.com/pod-product-compliance
Lightning Source LLC
Chambersburg PA
CBHW040101160426
43193CB00002B/39